Contents

Walk		Mile		
1	River & Stepping Stones Walk	2.6		
2	Hope Valley View Walk	4.2		
3	Offerton and River Walk	4.5		
4	Lees Hall & Old Chapel Walk	4.5	7.3	ɔ
5	Hathersage Moor Walk	4.6	7.4	2-3
6	Robin Hood's Cross Walk	5.0	8.5	3-4
7	Moor, Wood & River Walk	5.4	8.6	3
8	Stanage Edge Walk	5.4	8.6	4
9	Roman Fort Walk	5.9	9.5	2

The walks have been graded for difficulty with 1 being the easiest/flattest to 5 the most demanding in terms of ascents/descents: -

It is strongly recommended that walkers wear suitable clothing and footwear, appropriate to the walk and conditions that can sometimes be encountered on open moorland and exposed hillsides. This usually means walking boots, outer waterproof/windproof jacket and a type of walking trousers (not jeans) along with a warm sweater and other body clothing. A small day rucksack with some food/drink and your personal items are also strongly recommended.

The description of a route or track is not evidence of a right of way or right to roam. Any compass bearings shown in this book are given as magnetic bearings.

It is recommended that a compass and the following map be used in conjunction with this book.
Ordnance Survey Explorer No. OL1 The Peak District - Dark Peak Area also OL24 for walk No. 7.

To help shorten the text the following abbreviations have been used throughout: -

PF = Public Footpath	**LT** = Left	**S** = Start
PB = Public Bridleway	**RT** = Right	**P** = Park
CP = Car Park	**RD** = Road	**FB** = Footbridge

I hope you enjoy this selection of walks, which are spread throughout the Hope and Hathersage areas. Most are undulating but the majority are not too demanding, with excellent scenery and views from the hills. I hope you get as much pleasure from walking them as I did.

Brian Smailes

Walk 1 - River and Stepping Stones Walk
Walk Time - 1hr 20min   **Distance - 2.6miles/4.1km**
Start - GR. 230815 - Beside The George Hotel, Hathersage.
Comment: A very pleasant easy walk by the river. Caution in times of heavy rain and flood. Children should be supervised on the sometimes-narrow path by the river.

1. Cross the **RD** at the junction opposite The George Hotel in Hathersage, and follow the B6001 for 33yds. Turn immediately **RT** by the side of The Little John pub down Mill Lane. Continue down the lane keeping the stream on the **RT** then go under the railway bridge. Follow it round then just past a stone house on your **RT** and a gate with Nether Hall on it, turn onto a **PF** signposted Leadmill Bridge and walk along the track over fields.
2. You eventually go through a gate, emerging on the **RD** by the bridge over the river. Turn **RT** over the bridge then **RT** again at the far side through an opening to walk along by the river. A sign there points to Shatton. Keep the river on your **RT** as you continue along the edge of Goose Nest Wood. Cross two small **FB**s and go through several gates, staying by the river.
3. Continue until you see some stepping-stones and a sign for Offerton to the **LT**. On your **RT** is a row of stepping-stones crossing the river. Cross here with care and ascend the far side. Continue along the path close by the river. Go through an opening into the next field following the worn path, which gradually veers away from the river. Go through a small gate to the main **RD**.
4. Cross the busy **RD** with care and follow the **PF** sign opposite, crossing two fields diagonally to the **RD** through the housing estate. Turn **RT** on the **RD**, walking back into Hathersage to your starting point.

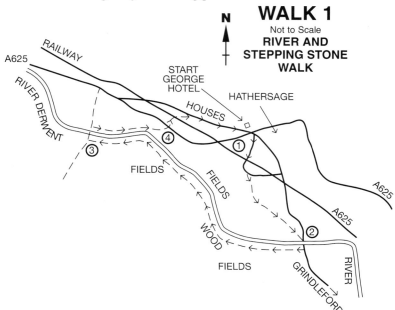

Walk 2 - Hope Valley View Walk
Walk Time - 2hrs 10mins   **Distance - 4.2miles/6.8km**
Start - GR. 207835 - Beside The Post Office in Bamford
Comment - A scenic walk with some short ascents/descents in the first half.

1. Opposite the Post Office is a **PF** sign by Fiddlers Close. Follow this to walk between the houses on a narrow path to a field and then to a lane. Cross the lane and go through a small gate to ascend the middle of the field bearing **RT** to a small gate then **FB** leading into the woodland. Ascend through the woodland; through a kissing gate then up a flight of steps to an access **RD** leading to the water works.

2. Turn **RT** on the **RD**, descending to a **PF** sign at the corner of the metal fence. Turn **LT** off the **RD**, walking around the perimeter fence and passing a bungalow on your **RT** then the entrance to the water works. Now follow the tarmac path in same direction to descend a flight of steps through the wood, crossing the stream at the bottom.

3. Ascend to a track through the wood and turn **RT**. Descend for a short distance and look for a small gate on your **LT** side, ascending five steps to it. Continue ascending following yellow arrows through the wood then over a field to emerge on Hurstclough Lane. Turn **RT** on the lane and walk 25yds to a **PF** sign on **RT** leading through a gate to Nether Hurst. Follow the path along and through the double metal gates to walk between the houses to the far side.

4. At far side, where the track meets another, look for a sign and stile leading into a field at the junction.

5. Descend the field to the bottom, crossing the bridge where it may be wet and ascend the narrow path on the far side to the top by a gate. The path bears **RT** to a gate leading onto a lane. Do not go onto the lane, but go through another gate, which is nearby, leading towards Thorpe Farm. Cross the field to the **LT** of the farm buildings. Cross the stile and further stiles, ascending the hillside to a small gate on **RT**.

6. You are now on the topside of a hill. Descend the hillside leaving the tree line just to your **LT** and a farm below on your **RT**. You come to a gate by houses on your **LT**. Do not go through but continue descending to a minor **RD** lower down in the estate, crossing your path. Continue down a narrow opening between the houses, emerging on the main **RD** just before the village.

7. At the main **RD** beside Hillfoot Farm B&B, turn **RT** and walk along the pavement with care to the entrance to Thorpe Farm then cross the **RD** looking for a narrow opening in the tree line and go through a small gate there. Follow the path and yellow arrows to the riverbank and the stepping-stones across the river.

8. Cross the stepping-stones with care then turn **RT** along the riverbank going through several small gates before coming to a stile to emerge onto a **RD**. Turn **RT** on the **RD**, walking 25yds to the main **RD**, cross with care, then through a kissing gate onto a **PF** signed Thornhill and Yorkshire Bridge.

9. Follow the path round under the railway bridge and across the recreation ground onto a lane. Turn **RT** on the lane over a bridge then **LT** at the far side by an industrial unit. Stay on the path, which joins the main **RD**, and continue back into Bamford.

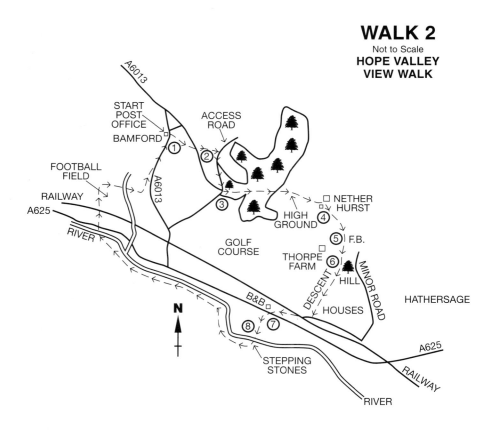

WALK 2

Not to Scale

HOPE VALLEY VIEW WALK

Walk 3 - Offerton and River Walk

Walk Time - 2hrs   **Distance - 4.5miles/7.2km**

Start - GR. 230815 - Beside The George Hotel, Hathersage.

Comment - A pleasant walk with one steep ascent to Offerton. Take care by the river.

1. Cross the **RD** at the junction beside The George Hotel in Hathersage and follow the B6001 for 33yds. Turn immediately **RT** by the side of The Little John pub down Mill Lane. Continue down the lane keeping the stream on the **RT** then go under the railway bridge. Follow it round then just past a stone house on your **RT** and a gate with Nether Hall on it, turn onto a **PF** signposted Leadmill Bridge and walk along the track over fields.

2. You eventually go through a gate, emerging on the **RD** by the bridge over the river. Turn **RT** over the bridge then **RT** again at the far side through an opening to walk along by the river. A sign there points to Shatton. Keep the river on your **RT** as you continue along the edge of Goose Nest Wood. Cross two small **FB**s and through several gates, staying by the river.

3. Continue until you see some stepping-stones and a sign for Offerton to the **LT** and turn **LT** there, crossing the field to ascend the hillside by a row of large trees. Ascend towards the buildings at the top of the hill, emerging on a lane by the buildings. Turn **LT** on the lane and continue ascending the winding lane and pass Offerton Hall. Stay on the metalled lane and walk along a straight section above the buildings. Good view off to your **LT**.

4. Look for a **PF** sign on **LT** 400yds after the bend in the **RD**. Cross the wooden step stile and descend the path between the bracken. Cross a stile further down the hillside as you approach some houses on the gradually descending path. You emerge on an access track by the houses, bear **LT** through a small gate. Look for the yellow arrow as you descend through a small gate and down some steps.

5. Descend a field into Callow Wood, on the worn path and continue descending the track through the wood to a kissing gate at the far end. Continue on the track through the field. You emerge on an access track and turn **RT** following it round as it ascends slightly. On reaching Mount Pleasant and the access **RD** there, turn **LT** through a small gate and continue across the field following the yellow arrow to the corner of the wood ahead.

6. Continue keeping the wood on your **LT** and on reaching the stone steps over the wall, cross and walk down the short path to the river below. On reaching the river, turn **RT** and walk back to the bridge and B6001 **RD**. Turn **LT** over the bridge and continue ascending the **RD**, which will take you back to your original starting point.

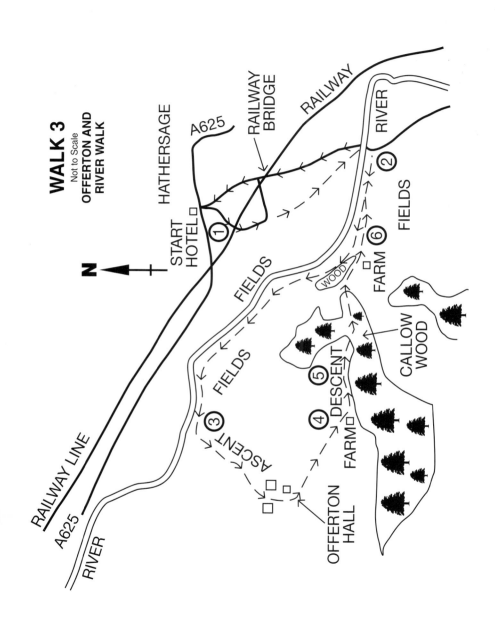

WALK 3
Not to Scale
OFFERTON AND RIVER WALK

N

START
HOTEL

HATHERSAGE

A625

RAILWAY BRIDGE

RAILWAY

RIVER

① ②

⑥ FARM

FIELDS

FIELDS

WOOD

FIELDS

FIELDS

③

ASCENT

④ FARM

DESCENT

⑤

OFFERTON HALL

CALLOW WOOD

RAILWAY LINE

A625

RIVER

Walk 4 - Lees Hall and Old Chapel Walk
Walk Time - 2hrs 35mins   **Distance - 4.53miles/7.3km**
Start - GR. 232815 - Beside the Royal Bank of Scotland, Hathersage.
Comment - A very historically interesting walk with some steep ascents/descents throughout.

1. Walk between Royal Bank of Scotland and CCC Outdoor shop following a **PF** sign to walk behind the houses. The path goes along the side of the cricket field. Keep the stream on your **LT**. Continue through two openings then where the path divides, bear **RT** following the yellow arrow and walking away from the river.

2. Cross the field diagonally towards some houses, cross a cattle grid and walk past the houses now on Balk Lane. Go through three wooden gates on the track as it gently ascends then you see a farm ahead and a training centre off to your **LT**. Follow the small wooden sign bearing **LT** down towards the training centre. Go through a small gate onto a path to emerge on Birley Lane.

3. Turn **RT** on the lane walking past the house on **LT** then a short distance further turn **LT** at a **PF** sign pointing up a driveway to North Lees Estate. Continue steeply up the drive to North Lees Hall and as you pass it, turn **RT** up some steps and through a farm gate. A path bears **LT** and ahead. Take the **LT** path and walk approx. 100yds to a small stone with arrows on it.

4. Turn **LT** there, then after 15yds cross stone steps over a wall. Turn **LT** now to descend a path through the bracken, leaving North Lees Farm off to your **LT**. You should see houses on the hillside ahead. This is Greens House, which you pass. The remains of an old chapel is nearby. Cross a stile then stepping-stones over the stream. Follow the track round to Greens House.

5. Cross fields as you approach the houses before going through a wooden 5-bar gate to walk along the side of the houses. Cross a cattle grid at the far side and walk up the access track, crossing another cattle grid by another house as you emerge on the **RD**. Bear **RT** on the **RD** then immediately **LT** through a kissing gate, following a **PF** sign.

6. Cross the field and stone steps, continuing down the field then over a wooden stile, which takes you nearby Upper Hurst Farm. Continue over fields, crossing stiles to Gatehouse then on to Hurstclough Lane. Turn **RT** on Hurstclough Lane and follow along to a **PF** on **LT**. Go through a small wooden gate and walk along the grass path parallel with the lane then turn back onto the lane.

7. Where the lane forks take the **RT** fork, which descends to a **PF** sign pointing back towards Nether Hurst. Turn **LT** there through a gate and walk along towards the houses. Walk between the houses on the access track and where the track meets another at the far side, look for a sign and stile leading into a field at the junction.

8. Descend the field to the bottom, crossing the bridge where it may be wet and ascend the narrow path on the far side to the top by a gate. The path bears **RT** to a gate leading onto a lane. Do not go onto the lane, but go through another gate, which is nearby, leading towards Thorpe Farm. Cross the field to the **LT** of the farm buildings. Cross the stile and further stiles, ascending the hillside to a small gate on **RT**.

9. You are now on the topside of a hill. Descend the hillside leaving the tree line just to your **LT** and a farm below on your **RT**. You come to a gate by houses on your **LT**. Do not go through but continue descending to a minor **RD** lower down in the estate, crossing your path. Turn **LT** and walk back now in the direction of Hathersage, emerging on the main **RD** just before the village. Continue into Hathersage returning to your start point.

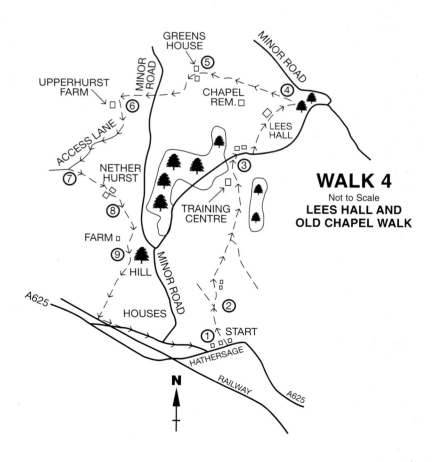

Walk 5 - Hathersage Moor Walk
Walk Time - 2hrs   **Distance - 4.6miles/7.4km**
Start - GR. 266802 - Fox House Inn
Comment - A pleasant walk with good views and more gentle ascents/descents

1. From the Fox House Inn continue back round the bend of the main A625 **RD** towards Hathersage and take the minor **RD** off to your **LT** 100yds further round. You come to a white gate on your **RT** after another 100yds, opposite a lodge. Go through and continue on the path through the wood, to the far end, emerging on the main **RD** at the bend by Burbage Bridge on the A625.
2. Turn **LT** on the **RD** and walk over the bridge, ignoring the first **PF** on your **RT**, take the second one further along. Turn **RT** here over a stile onto a grass path and ascend on the grass then stony path. As you near the top of the hill there is a stony path on **RT**. Take this, walking to a large sheepfold at GR. 253816. Bear **LT** round it and head towards the large rocks on the hillside ahead. The path winds round towards the **RD**.
3. In front of the large rocks, continue on the path, where you may see the cement works and views down the valley. Cross a stile onto the **RD**, turn **RT** and walk for 370yds to another stile further up on **RT**. Cross this and walk up to Higger Tor. Do not take the path off to **LT** but continue ahead to descend between the large rocks onto a path at the far side.
4. Follow the path towards the next large rock outcrop and just before it, turn **LT** to descend on a narrow path to the **RT** of the wood below and over the small packhorse bridge there. Ascend the far side onto a definite track further up then turn **RT** and descend gradually back to Burbage Bridge at the bend in the **RD**.
5. Cross straight over onto a path, through a kissing gate. Follow the path back to the small gate by the white farm gate. Turn **LT** along the **RD** to the junction then **RT** on the pavement back to the Fox House Inn.

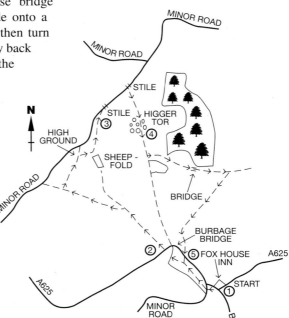

WALK 5
Not to Scale
HATHERSAGE MOOR WALK

Walk 6 - Robin Hood's Cross Walk
Walk Time - 2hrs 45mins Distance - 5.3miles/8.5km
Start - GR. 171835 - Main CP in Hope
Comment - A pleasant walk over fields and a steady but steep ascent to Robin Hoods Cross giving excellent views over a wide area. A steep descent back, but worth the effort.

1. Leaving the **CP** in Hope, turn **RT**, walking to the Woodroffe Arms then turn **RT** to walk between the pub and the church. Walk down the **RD** then branch **LT** along Forres **RD** looking for a stile beside a seat on **LT**. Cross and follow path across fields and stiles passing the Roman Fort of Anavio.

2. Descend the field to emerge on a **RD** through a kissing gate and turn **LT**. Cross the stone bridge then take your 1st **RT** beside an old barn and walk along Brough Lane on a steep ascent. The route turns into a stony track as you continue ascending; there are good views of Bradwell to the **RT**. Pass the entrance to Ellmore Hill Farm as you continue along the stony track.

3. Nearing a hill on your **RT**, you come to a metal farm gate across the track. Turn **RT** before it, over the stone step stile. Continue on a grass path keeping the wall to your **LT** and go through an opening into the next field then through another opening as you look down on the village of Bradwell. You start to descend the hillside on a narrow steep path with the wall on your **LT**.

4. Continue on the long steep descent to a gate at the bottom. You emerge onto an access lane by a house. Continue descending into Bradwell, emerging by the houses. Follow the narrow **RD** between the houses. Walk down Bessie Lane then go through an opening to descend some steps to the main **RD** through Bradwell. Continuing through Bradwell, just past the church is a small bridge over the stream. Turn **RT** just before the bridge.

5. Walk 150yds along the lane to a **PF** sign on **RT**. Follow it and you soon go through an opening into a field then through a series of fields. As you are nearing Brough, your path turns **LT** for 45yds then **RT** to emerge at the **RD** junction in Brough. Just before the main **RD** you come to St.Anne's Well, dating from 1859. At the traffic lights at Brough, turn **LT** to walk back on the pavement into Hope.

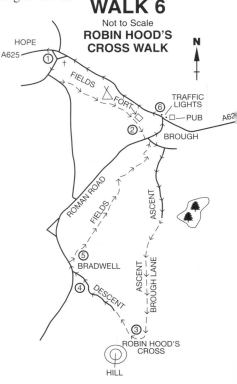

WALK 6
Not to Scale
ROBIN HOOD'S
CROSS WALK
N

HOPE
A625
FIELDS
FORT
TRAFFIC LIGHTS
PUB
A62
BROUGH
ROMAN ROAD
FIELDS
ASCENT
ASCENT
BROUGH LANE
BRADWELL
DESCENT
ROBIN HOOD'S CROSS
HILL

Walk 7 - Moor, Wood & River Walk
Walk Time - 2hrs 45mins   **Distance - 5.4miles/8.7km**
Start - GR. 234814 - Park on Crossland RD in Hathersage at the top of the village.
Comment - One steep ascent/descent and some smaller ones on this walk, which takes in wood, moor and river.

1. From Crossland **RD**, turn **RT** on the main **RD** walking away from Hathersage to a **PF** on **LT** between the houses. You pass more houses as you ascend the lane. The track merges into a path as you continue passing a white house. Go through a gate and take the middle path rising steeply through the trees. The path soon bears **RT** and continues ascending. Follow it along the **RT** side of the wood. Leaving the wood, continue straight ahead now keeping the stone boundary wall on your **LT** walking up to Scraperlow (house) at the top.
2. Just as you get there you come to the corner of a stone wall, cross the steps there following the signs to take you in front of Scraperlow (a splendid looking house). As you walk to it, you see a **PF** sign on your **RT**, follow it in front of the farmhouse and walk straight across the centre of the field to cross a stile at the far side. This brings you to Mitchell Field.
3. Turn **RT** at Mitchell Field and ascend to the **RD** and ascend again to the next **RD** above. Cross the **RD** and over a stile before ascending the short distance to a track. Turn **RT** on the track, following it down towards a prominent rock feature called Over Owler Tor. The path takes you just to the **RT** of it then you come to a stile and fence. Do not cross the stile but pass it, now keeping the wire fence on your **RT** as you walk down to the **RD** at GR. 249800
4. Just before the main **RD**, go through a kissing gate and walk to the bend in the **RD**. Cross with care and follow the path on the far side, crossing a stile to continue, with care, along the top side of the cliff and passing the climbers area. A wire fence is on your **LT**. Walk **RT** to the far end where there is a stone wall on your **LT**. Continue on a narrow path through the bracken between the wall and the edge of the rock face.
5. The path then descends to a gate then steeply down over a stile and down to a path running **LT** to **RT** through the wood. Turn **RT** and continue on the stone path down to Grindleford Station, passing through a gate near houses. Continue on the access lane before arriving at Padley Hall (ancient monument) and after a short distance look for a kissing gate on your **LT** leading over a railway bridge and down towards the river.

6. Now on a grass path you see a sign 'Leadmill', follow it over fields and into Coppice Wood. Continue on the path through the wood as you approach the river. Continue on the main path back towards Hathersage. You emerge on an access track and continue along to the main bridge over the river.

7. When you come to the bridge, turn **RT** and walk on the pavement into Hathersage. Just under the railway bridge, take the **RD** on the **RT**, (not the one to the station) and ascend Back Lane to return to your starting point.

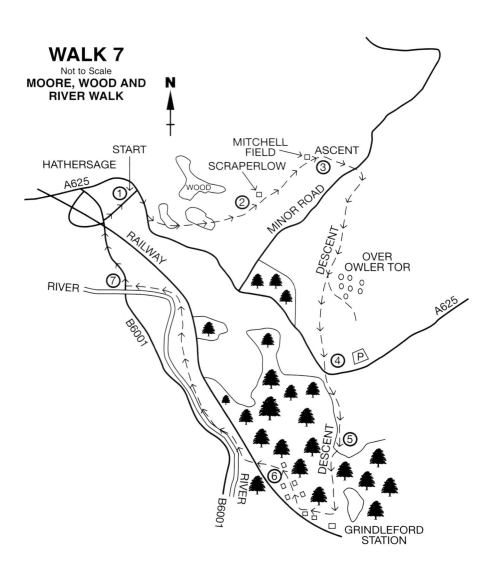

WALK 7
Not to Scale
MOORE, WOOD AND RIVER WALK

N

Walk 8 - Stanage Edge Walk
Walk Time - 2hrs 10mins   **Distance - 5.4miles/8.65km**
Start - GR. 234819 - Entrance to Hathersage Parish Church
Comment - A walk with very good views but can be very windy on the exposed top and a lot of ascent/descents.

1. Leaving the entrance to Hathersage Church, turn **LT** to the top corner of the churchyard and look for the **PF** sign and stile beside a metal farm gate. Cross and walk on a grass path to a marker post with yellow arrows. Turn **LT** there and descend the field, crossing the brook at the bottom. Ascend the next field keeping the hedge line on your **LT**.

2. The path forks part way up, take the **RT** fork and ascend the grass path and cross a stile heading towards a wood. You pass just above Cowclose Farm then enter a field before descending to a **RD** at the far side. On reaching the **RD** turn **RT** and continue up the **RD** to cross two cattle grids, as you cross the 2nd one, turn **LT** at the **RD** junction.

3. Follow the **RD** round to the public toilets, turn **RT** just before them onto a path and head up towards the wood, going through a gate into the wood. You leave the wood at the far side and stay on the path as you ascend on the stone path onto Stanage Edge. On the top, turn **RT** and follow path along keeping away from the edge. Continue until you reach the 'trig' point and turn **RT** just before it on a path descending to the **RD**.

4. On reaching the **RD**, turn **LT** and walk along looking for a stile on the **RT**. Cross and walk towards a 2nd **RD**, 30yds before it turn **RT** and follow the grass track which initially runs parallel with the **RD**. Continue **RT** to the bottom where you emerge on a bend in a **RD**. Turn **LT** and continue down the **RD** for 500yds to a metal farm gate on your **RT** and ascend a track towards Toothill Farm.

5. As you approach the farm, go through a 5-bar gate and walk to the front of the farm where you bear **LT** on the descending path towards the church which you may see below. Continue on the winding path then onto a lane by houses, to emerge just below the church. Ascend the **RD** back to the church.

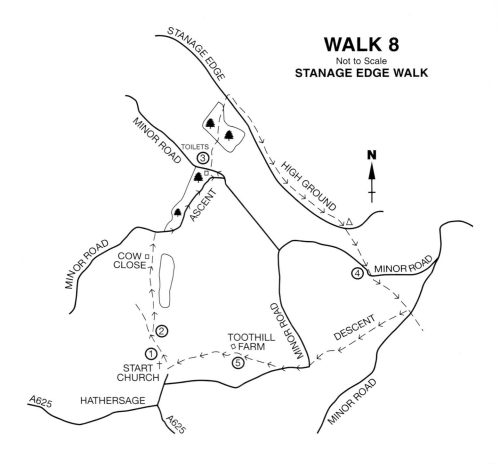

WALK 8

Not to Scale

STANAGE EDGE WALK

STANAGE EDGE

MINOR ROAD

HIGH GROUND

N

TOILETS

③

ASCENT

MINOR ROAD

COW CLOSE

②

MINOR ROAD

④   MINOR ROAD

DESCENT

TOOTHILL FARM

⑤

MINOR ROAD

①

START CHURCH

HATHERSAGE

A625

A625

MINOR ROAD

Walk - 9 - Roman Fort Walk
Walk Time - 3hrs 20mins   **Distance - 5.9miles/9.5km**
Start - GR. 171835 - Main CP in Hope
Comment - A nice walk over fields with not much climbing and good scenery.

1. Turn **RT** out of the **CP** in Hope, and walk along the main **RD** to Aston Lane where a sign states 'Aston only', on **LT**. Walk along Aston Lane under the railway bridge then take 1st **RT** following **PF** sign. Go through an opening at the side of a metal farm gate and cross the field diagonally **LT** to a stile by another farm gate.

2. Just past here you cross another **PF** but keep in the same direction, crossing another stile then over a small **FB** and another stile there. Ascend the next field to another stile, cross a **RD** then cross another stile beside Hallam Barn. Continue on an access lane past Round Meadow Barn. Look for a stile beside a wooden 5-bar gate just before a farmhouse. Cross the field to a telegraph pole then go through a gate.

3. Cross a small **FB** following the worn path along the side of a field. You cross a stile onto the access lane. Continue along the lane, ignoring the footpath on the **LT**, until you see a metal gate on both sides of the lane, look for a small wooden gate hidden behind a bush on your **LT**. Go through then turn **RT**, walking parallel with the narrow lane.

4. Follow the yellow arrows and cross a stile then through a narrow strip of woodland, followed by a gate at the far side. Go through a wooden 5-bar gate and through another at the far side of the access track which leads to a farm on **LT**. Go through an opening at the side of a metal gate, keeping the hedge on your **RT**. Continue along the next field by the hedge.

5. Go through a wooden 5-bar gate and continue towards a cluster of cottages, keeping the wire fence on your **RT**. You emerge on an access **RD** just before the cottages, turning **LT** then **RT** to walk behind an old barn. Cross a stile behind the cottages and follow the narrow worn path gradually descending on a flight of steps to a 4-way signpost. Follow the sign to Bamford, descending just to the **RT** of a house. Go through a gate in front of the house onto a **RD**.

6. Cross the **RD** to a stile next to a **PF** sign as you now descend steeply. Cross the stile to a footpath and cross it following the sign for Touchstone Trail. Cross another stile, still descending steeply. At the bottom of the hill, you come to a track where you turn **RT** through an opening next to a wooden gate with a barn in front.

7. Pass the barn then bear **LT** through an opening and cross the field diagonally. Cross a stile beside a wooden 5-bar gate and cross next field diagonally following the worn grass path towards a large mill building. Go through a gate as you arrive at the waterfall and river at Bamford Mill. Cross the **FB** and follow path round by the mill. You emerge on a **RD**; turning **RT** follow it round, passing houses on the way to the main **RD** in Bamford.

8. Turn **RT** here, walking on Station **RD** for a short distance to a gate on **RT** leading towards some workshops. Pass the 1st workshop then cross a bridge on **RT**. Walk along the lane and as you come to a large house on **RT**, turn **LT**, following sign for Shatton. Cross the stile there and walk along field keeping hedge on **RT**. Go under a railway bridge and emerge on main **RD**.

9. Cross the **RD** and cross a small stone bridge to ascend the wide **RD** between the houses. Turn **RT** along the next cul-de-sac and continue to a stile in top **LT** corner. Follow worn path across fields and cross several stiles and pass a barn, all in same direction. The path merges with the narrow **RD** there where you turn **RT**.

10. Follow the path running parallel with the narrow lane. At a bend 85yds further on, turn **RT** through a 5-bar gate following the track. Halfway along the track is a signpost pointing **RT** across the field. Cross the field then descend towards the river. Cross a stile and descend steeply now keeping the wire fence to your **RT** as you head towards the **RD** and river. Cross a stile with a large house ahead and continue across the field.

11. Go through a small metal gate on the **RT** side of the house near the river. Cross stone steps and emerge on the **RD** opposite an agricultural merchant. Turn **LT** along the **RD** and cross a small bridge after 200yds then turn **RT** following a **PF** signposted Hope and Castleton, passing an old Roman fort called Anavio. Cross a ladder stile and continue through into next field, passing the plaque for the fort. Cross a **FB** continuing in same direction over fields and stiles to eventually descend to the **RD**.

12. Turn **RT** and descend the **RD** to another **RD**. Turn **RT** again to descend towards the church in Hope then **LT** at the junction back to the **CP**.

WALK 9

Not to Scale

ROMAN FORT WALK

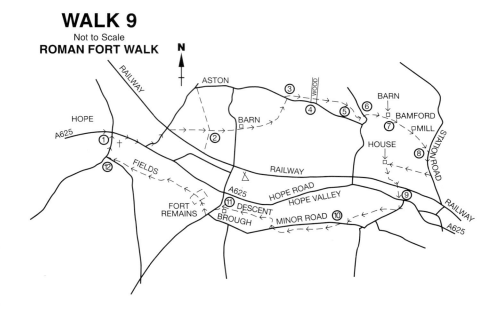